University of Chester

This book is to be returned on or before the last date stamped below. Overdue charges will be incurred by the late return of books.

Nelson

Book 3 – Contents

This symbol shows that you need to correct mistakes in the text.

Nouns

Proper nouns are special names.

Capital letters are used for **proper nouns**.

Paul

Wales

February

We use capital letters for titles that go with the names of people.

Miss Husain

Doctor Evans

Major Lewis

We use capital letters for the first letter of the first word and other important words in the titles of books, films and plays.

Remember!
Conjunctions are joining words.
Prepositions tell you where something is.

James and the **G**iant **P**each

Star **W**ars

The articles **a, an** and **the**, prepositions such as **in** and **on**, and conjunctions such as **and** and **but** usually don't need capitals.

Write these names correctly in your book.

1 lord lambeth
2 mrs kelly
3 bishop jones
4 sir roger gray
5 queen elizabeth
6 prince john
7 colonel crisp
8 lady mary smith
9 judge wright
10 mr harris

Write these titles, putting in the **capital letters**.

1 alice in wonderland   a book

2 the secret garden   a book

3 toy story   a film

4 the wind in the willows   a book

5 the empire strikes back   a film

6 romeo and juliet   a play

Copy this story.
Put in the **capital letters**.

jeremy had just finished reading a book called the owl who was afraid of the dark. he went to the library to choose a new book. he met his friend lee.

"have you read midnight adventure?" asked lee.

"no, but i have seen the film," said jeremy. "it didn't have the same title. i think it was called treasure hunt. let's ask mrs jenkins if the book is in the library."

mrs jenkins was not at the desk but mr karim helped the boys to find the book.

Remember! You need capital letters to begin sentences.

Adjectives

Adjectives are describing words, which tell us more about a person, place or thing.

a **happy** child   a **vast** desert   a **muddy** boot

Numbers can be adjectives.
Number adjectives describe the **number** of nouns.

three chairs   **ten** hours

Number order adjectives to 10 are: first, second, third, fourth, fifth, sixth, seventh, eighth, ninth, tenth.

Number adjectives can also describe the **order** of nouns.

the **first** prize   the **second** trumpet

GRAMMAR *Focus*

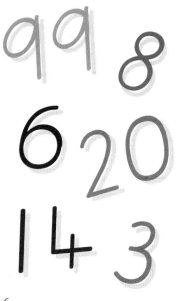

Match the **adjectives** which tell you the **number** of nouns with the **adjectives** which tell you the **order** of nouns. Write the pairs in your book.

six	fourteenth
three	eighth
twenty	sixth
ninety-nine	twentieth
fourteen	third
eight	ninety-ninth

6

A Copy the sentences below.
Underline the **number adjectives**.
Draw rings around the **nouns** they describe.

1 There are four glasses on the table.

2 We saw two seagulls on the sand.

3 I got ten answers right.

4 My coat has six pockets.

5 We need two eggs and one lemon to make the pancakes.

B Copy the sentences below.
Underline the **number order adjectives**.
Draw rings around the **nouns** they describe.

1 The sixteenth day of June is a Monday.

2 The fourth book on the shelf is blue.

3 The old lady is in her eightieth year.

4 That's the tenth time I've told you.

5 The fifth boat in the race sank.

Look at the picture.
Complete the sentences using **number order adjectives**.

Six children were in the running race. Ned was the _____ to cross the winning line but Claire was a close _____ . Dave came in _____ and Bob was _____ . Nora and Ian were placed _____ and _____ at the end of the race.

Singular and plural

Singular means 'one person or thing'.
Plural means 'more than one person or thing'.
To make a noun plural, we usually add **s**.

one mask two mask**s**

To make nouns ending in **s**, **ch**, **sh** and **x** plural, we add **es**.

two bus**es** three watch**es** four bush**es** five fox**es**

When a noun ends in **y**, we have to take off the **y** and add **ies**.

one pony two pon**ies** one baby two bab**ies**

If the letter in front of the **y** is a vowel, we just add **s**.

> Remember!
> The vowels are: **a**, **e**, **i**, **o** and **u**.

one toy two toy**s**

GRAMMAR *Focus*

> Remember!
> Add **s** or **es**, or take off the **y** and add **ies**.

In your book, write the **plurals** of these words.

1 flask   2 class   3 disaster   4 spot
5 tray   6 church   7 hobby   8 fly
9 flash   10 lorry   11 baby   12 day

Remember the capital letters and full stops.

A Write the **plurals** of these words.

1 lady   2 puppy   3 lily   4 city

B Put each of the **plural words** from part A into a sentence of your own.

C Write the **singular** of these words.

1 cherries   2 armies   3 bays   4 diaries

D Put each of your **singular words** from part C into a sentence of your own.

GRAMMAR *Extension*

Use a word ending in **s**, **es** or **ies** to complete each of the following sentences.

1 Small horses are called _____.

2 Big roads for fast moving traffic are called _____.

3 _____ let out smoke from the roofs of houses.

4 _____ are areas of low land between hills.

5 _____ are used to lock doors.

6 When the weather is hot, people often eat ice _____.

7 You strike _____ to make fire.

8 Very young children are called _____.

UNIT 4

Prepositions

A **preposition** is a word that shows the relationship of a noun or a pronoun to another word in a sentence.

Prepositions often tell us about **position**.

The squirrel is **in** the tree.

The boy ran **after** the ball.

Sam was cross **with** the dog.

The bird took the food **from** the table.

GRAMMAR *Focus*

A Copy the following sentences into your book. Underline the **prepositions**.

1 The rope was tied around the tree.

2 It was cooler when the sun went behind the clouds.

3 It was very windy during the night.

4 The path went through the woods.

5 The duck flew across the lake.

B Copy the **prepositions** below.
Choose the opposite of each one from the prepositions in the box. Write down the pairs of prepositions.

with above up on far inside before under

1 outside 2 down 3 below 4 after

5 without 6 over 7 near 8 off

10

Remember the capital letters and full stops.

A Choose the correct **preposition** to finish each sentence.

1 I am sorry about/for breaking the plate.

2 Black is the opposite to/of white.

3 We played football for/during two hours.

4 No one knew the cause of/for the accident.

5 Is this book different to/from that one?

B Use each of the following **prepositions** in a sentence of your own.

1 between   2 behind   3 against

4 into   5 beside   6 towards

GRAMMAR *Extension*

One preposition is used twice.

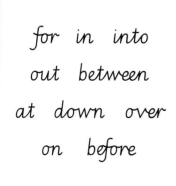

for   in   into
out   between
at   down   over
on   before

Copy the passage below.
Use the **prepositions** from the box to fill the gaps.

Martin came _____ at four o'clock. He put his jacket _____ the chair and took some bread _____ of the cupboard. He put butter _____ two slices and put jam _____ them. He poured milk _____ a glass and sat _____ on the chair to eat his sandwich. Martin looked _____ the clock. He would have to wait _____ ten minutes _____ his friends came to call _____ him.

Sentences

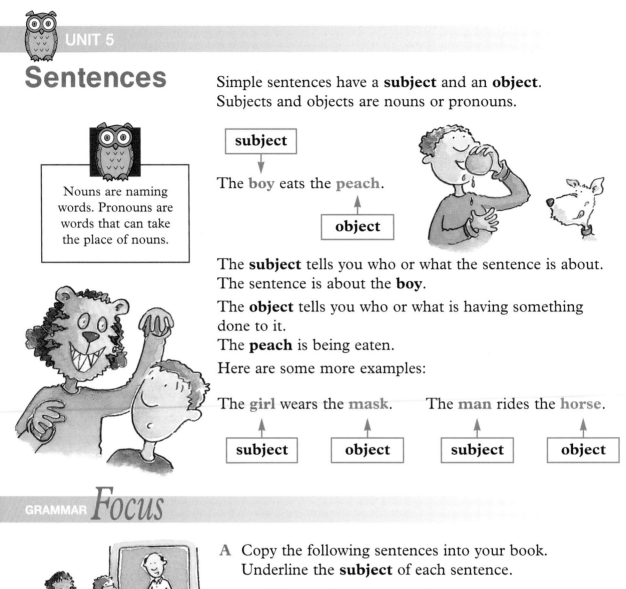

Nouns are naming words. Pronouns are words that can take the place of nouns.

Simple sentences have a **subject** and an **object**. Subjects and objects are nouns or pronouns.

subject

The **boy** eats the **peach**.

object

The **subject** tells you who or what the sentence is about. The sentence is about the **boy**.

The **object** tells you who or what is having something done to it.
The **peach** is being eaten.

Here are some more examples:

The **girl** wears the **mask**.   The **man** rides the **horse**.

subject	object	subject	object

GRAMMAR *Focus*

A Copy the following sentences into your book. Underline the **subject** of each sentence.

1 We are buying tickets.

2 I bought a jacket.

3 The squirrel ate the nuts.

B Copy the following sentences into your book. Underline the **object** of each sentence.

1 The nurse wore a uniform.

2 The bus crashed into a tree.

3 The cars are in the garage.

Finish these sentences by adding an interesting **object** to each one.

1 The old dog ran into the _____ .

2 My Dad mends _____ .

3 Harry and Lucy walked _____ .

4 The rocket flew _____ .

5 The giraffe ate _____ .

GRAMMAR *Extension*

A Make these sentences more interesting by putting an **adjective** in front of each **object**.

1 I saw a snake.

2 Mum bought a pillow.

3 The man escaped from the prison.

4 The wind blew around the house.

5 Ella broke the window.

Adjectives are describing words.

B Write sentences of your own using these pairs of **subjects** and **objects**.

	Subject	Object
1	we	ball
2	the rain	garden
3	the crowd	train
4	the children	park
5	they	kitten

13

Pronouns

A **pronoun** can be used instead of a noun.

The candle is burning.
It is burning.

Rex hates cabbage.
He hates cabbage.

Here is a list of useful pronouns:

I	you	he	she	it	we	they
me	yourself	him	her	itself	us	them
myself	yourselves	himself	herself		ourselves	themselves

GRAMMAR *Focus*

Choose **pronouns** from the box to replace the brown words in the sentences below.
Write the correct pronouns in your book.

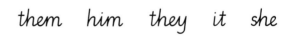

them   him   they   it   she

1   The vase fell on the floor and **the vase** broke.

2   The zebras wanted to drink so **the zebras** went to the water hole.

3   I told the children we would meet **the children** at ten o'clock.

4   The headmaster said I should come in to see **the headmaster**.

5   Denise ate quickly so **Denise** could go out early.

Use a **pronoun** from the box to finish each sentence.

| myself |
| yourself |
| himself |
| herself |
| itself |

1 Tara wants to paint the cottage _____ .

2 The dog stretched _____ in front of the fire.

3 The postman hurt _____ when he fell off his bike.

4 I want to go to the shops by _____ .

5 You almost cut _____ with that knife.

GRAMMAR *Extension*

A Change the **nouns** and **proper nouns** in these sentences into **pronouns**.
The first one is done for you.

1 Paula and Alex saw the ghost.

They saw _it_ .

2 Rachel waited for the milkman.

_____ waited for _____ .

3 Nigel and I waved to Scott.

_____ waved to _____ .

4 Edward met his friends.

_____ met _____ .

B Use each of these **pronouns** in sentences of your own.

1 yourself   2 they   3 myself

4 her   5 us   6 itself

Sentences

Direct speech is when we write the actual words that someone has spoken.

Direct speech can be written in speech bubbles like this:

If we want to write this as conversation, we need to use **inverted commas**.

We put **"** at the beginning of the words that are spoken and **"** at the end.

> "Lovely fresh cabbages!" shouted the man.
> "I'll have two please," said the woman.

Inverted commas are also called speech marks.

GRAMMAR *Focus*

A Find the **spoken words** in each sentence.
Copy them into your book.

1 "I must cut the grass today," said Mum.

2 "I'll be lucky to finish this homework," said Toby.

3 Mr Visram said, "My leg is very painful."

4 "Stick out your tongue," said the doctor.

B Copy these sentences.
Put **inverted commas** around the **spoken words**.

1 This window is broken, said the angry man.

2 I have lost my lunchbox, said the girl.

3 Marion said, I want a drink.

4 The clown said, I like making people laugh.

Find the words that are spoken. Put " in front of them and " at the end.

Look at this conversation:

"Are you frightened?" asked the ghost.

"No," said the little boy.

"You should be frightened. I'm a ghost. I frighten people."

"Well, you don't frighten me," said the boy.

The spoken words have **inverted commas** around them.

When a different person speaks, we **start a new line**.

Copy the conversation below.

Put **inverted commas** around the spoken words and **start a new line** when a different person speaks.

Did you see the rabbit go down that hole? said the farmer. No, said Mary. Look over there by that big tree, said the farmer. Oh yes! The rabbit has just popped out again, said Mary. It might not be the same one. There are lots of rabbits in that hole, said the farmer.

GRAMMAR *Extension*

Remember to put inverted commas around the spoken words.

Always using the word **said** in conversations is not very interesting.

Below are some words you can use instead of **said**.

Write a **direct speech sentence** using each one.

1 *cried* 2 *called* 3 *shouted*

4 *asked* 5 *muttered* 6 *whispered*

Nouns

A **noun** is the name of a person, place or thing.

boy   house   box

A **collective noun** is a special name for a group of people, places or things.

Collective nouns tell us the name of a **collection** of things.

a **swarm** of bees   a **fleet** of ships

GRAMMAR *Focus*

Choose a word from the box to go with each of the **collective nouns** below.
Write them in your book.

books	wolves	flowers
sheep	cows	trees

1 a forest of _____

2 a herd of _____

3 a bunch of _____

4 a flock of _____

5 a pack of _____

6 a library of _____

18

A What would you expect to find in each of these groups?

1 an army   2 a crew   3 a pride

4 an orchestra   5 a bouquet   6 a gaggle

> Sometimes we use the same collective noun for different things.

B Find two things for each of these **collective nouns**.

1 a pack of _____

2 a herd of _____

3 a bunch of _____

4 a flock of _____

5 a string of _____

GRAMMAR *Extension*

A Copy the sentences.
Fill each gap with a **collective noun**.

1 The boy ran up the _____ of stairs.

2 The _____ of people gathered outside the cinema.

3 The _____ clapped at the end of the play.

4 The _____ of fish escaped from the fishing net.

5 The _____ scored two goals to win the football match.

B Choose five **collective nouns** and put each one into a sentence of your own.

Check-up 1

Proper nouns

A In your book, write these names correctly.

1 tina robinson
2 richard smith
3 kamal khan
4 doctor finch

B Write these book titles correctly.

1 a tale of two cities
2 the twits
3 the railway children
4 the silver sword

Adjectives

A Copy the sentences below.
Underline the **number adjectives**.

1 Five ponies are in the field.
2 Six thousand people watched the match.
3 I planted twenty trees.

B Use these **number order adjectives** in sentences of your own.

1 eighth
2 fortieth
3 thirty-second

Singular and plural

Write the **plurals** of these words.

1 berry
2 key
3 post
4 penny
5 ruby
6 kidney

Prepositions

A Copy the sentences below.
Fill each gap with a **preposition**.

1 The bird flew _____ the trees.
2 I will hide _____ the shed.
3 "It is very cold _____ ." said Mum.

B Use each of these **prepositions** in a sentence of your own.

1 beneath
2 around
3 during

Sentences

A Copy the following sentences.
Underline the **subject** of each sentence.

1 The goat ate the grass.

2 We like to ride our bicycles.

3 The circus came to town.

B Copy the following sentences.
Underline the **object** of each sentence.

1 Mrs Potter cleaned the windows.

2 Freda ate an ice cream.

3 I like oranges.

C Copy these sentences.
Put **inverted commas** around the **spoken words**.

1 Let me bathe that cut, said the nurse.

2 The boy muttered, I always get the blame.

3 What a mess, Mum shouted.

4 I'm very cold, moaned the little girl.

Pronouns

Copy the sentences below.
Underline the **pronouns**.

1 I am going to tidy the garage myself.

2 He watched the seagull as it dived for
the fish.

3 When you go out, see if you can see it.

4 You must get yourself ready in good time.

Collective nouns

Use the following **collective nouns** in sentences of
your own.

1 herd   2 band   3 bundle   4 queue

Singular and plural

Singular means 'one person or thing'.
Plural means 'more than one person or thing'.

To make a noun plural, we usually add **s**.

shadow – shadow**s**   rabbit – rabbit**s**

To make nouns ending in **s**, **ch**, **sh** and **x** plural, we add **es**.

glass – glass**es**   match – match**es**
flash – flash**es**   box – box**es**

When a noun ends in **y**, we take off the **y** and add **ies**.

body – bod**ies**   lorry – lorr**ies**

If the letter in front of the **y** is a vowel, we just add **s**.

chimney – chimney**s**   guy – guy**s**

Words ending in **f** and **fe** can be made plural by changing the **f** or **fe** to **v** and adding **es**.

wolf – wol**ves**   shelf – shel**ves**   knife – kni**ves**

Learn these examples:

calf – calves	elf – elves	half – halves
knife – knives	loaf – loaves	life – lives
scarf – scarves	sheaf – sheaves	shelf – shelves
thief – thieves	leaf – leaves	wolf – wolves

For some **f** and **fe** words, we just add **s**.

Some nouns ending in **f** or **fe** can have an **s** or a **ves** ending:

wharf can be **wharfs** or **wharves**

hoof can be **hoofs** or **hooves**.

Learn these examples:

chief – chiefs	cliff – cliffs	dwarf – dwarfs
gulf – gulfs	sheriff – sheriffs	waif – waifs
oaf – oafs	reef – reefs	roof – roofs
muff – muffs	handkerchief – handkerchiefs	

GRAMMAR *Focus*

In your book, write the **plurals** of these words.

1 scarf	2 reef	3 sheaf	4 life
5 thief	6 cliff	7 half	8 wife

A Write the **plurals** of the following words.

   1 leaf   2 loaf   3 shelf   4 chief

B Put each of the **plural words** from part A into a sentence of your own.

C Write the **singular** of the following words.

   1 hooves   2 wolves   3 safes   4 elves

D Put each of the **singular words** from part C into a sentence of your own.

GRAMMAR *Extension*

Use **plural words** ending in **ves** or **s** to finish the sentences below. The pictures will help you.

1 _____ grow on trees.

2 We use _____ for blowing our noses.

3 _____ are used for cutting.

4 People who steal things are called _____.

5 Horses have four _____.

6 _____ kept law and order in America's Wild West.

Adjectives

Adjectives are words that describe nouns.

long   small   short   cold

We use a **comparative adjective** to compare **two** things. To make an adjective into a comparative adjective, we usually add **er**.

This rope is long**er** than that rope.

We use a **superlative adjective** to compare **three or more** things.
To make an adjective into a superlative adjective, we usually add **est**.

This rope is the long**est** of the three.

For adjectives that end in **y**, we have to change the **y** to **i** before we add **er** or **est**.

windy	wind**ier**	wind**iest**
sleepy	sleep**ier**	sleep**iest**
lazy	laz**ier**	laz**iest**

If the adjective is a long word and does not end in **y**, we put the word '**more**' in front of it when we are comparing two things and '**most**' in front of it when we are comparing three or more things.

important	**more** important	**most** important
modern	**more** modern	**most** modern
frightening	**more** frightening	**most** frightening

GRAMMAR *Focus*

Copy this table into your book. Fill in the missing words.

Adjective	Comparative	Superlative
round	_____	roundest
_____	shorter	shortest
_____	heavier	_____
beautiful	_____	most beautiful
_____	more terrible	_____

A Copy the sentences below.
Make the red **adjectives** into **comparative adjectives**.

1 That question is *easy* than the last one.

2 It is *cloudy* than yesterday.

3 Our dog is *intelligent* than our cat.

B Copy the sentences below.
Make the red **adjectives** into **superlative adjectives**.

1 This is the *smelly* of all the cheeses.

2 He is the *lazy* boy in the school.

3 This is the *peaceful* place I have ever been.

GRAMMAR *Extension*

A Use the **comparative** or **superlative** of an adjective from the box to compare each set of things below. The first one has been done for you.

sunny	heavy	bumpy	tidy	ancient

1 compare the weight of two loaves

The white loaf is heavy.

The brown loaf is heavier.

2 compare the surface of two roads

3 compare the weather on three days

4 compare the age of three fossils

5 compare the neatness of two rooms

B Use these **comparative** and **superlative adjectives** in sentences of your own.

1 *messier*   2 *more nervous*

3 *cheekiest*   4 *most dangerous*

Verbs

Tense comes from the Latin word 'tempus', meaning 'time'.

When we use **verbs** to tell us about something that has happened in the past, we use the **past tense**.

To make the past tense, we usually add **ed** or **d** to the verb family name.

I comb**ed** my hair.   I wash**ed** my face.
I walk**ed** downstairs.   I pick**ed** up my bag.

Another way to make the past tense is like this:

Past tense of the verb 'to be'	+ verb	+ ing	
I was	sing	ing	= I **was singing**
you were	point	ing	= you **were pointing**
he was	help	ing	= he **was helping**
she was	laugh	ing	= she **was laughing**
it was	rain	ing	= it **was raining**
we were	jump	ing	= we **were jumping**
you were	shout	ing	= you **were shouting**
they were	fight	ing	= they **were fighting**

We use this way of writing the past tense when an action goes on for some time or something else happens at the same time.

I **was walking** to the shops when it started to rain.
We **were playing** football for three hours.
She **was reading** when the telephone rang.

GRAMMAR *Focus*

Copy the following sentences into your book.
Underline the two words in each sentence that make up the **past tense**.

1 The birds were flying around the garden.

2 The tree was bending in the wind.

3 The ducks were quacking for some food.

4 The dog was scattering leaves everywhere.

Remember! Use the past tense of the verb 'to be' and an 'ing' word.

Copy the sentences below.
Use the **past tense** instead of the verb family name.

1 Jill (to post) a letter when she saw her friend.

2 The children (to talk) until the teacher came in.

3 I (to hope) to cut the grass but it started to rain.

4 We had a power cut while we (to watch) the television.

GRAMMAR *Extension*

A Copy this table and fill in the missing **verbs**.

Verb family name	Past tense with 'ed or 'd'	Past tense with verb 'to be' + 'ing'
to look	looked	I was looking
to save	_____	we were _____
_____	laughed	he was _____
to show	_____	they _____ showing
_____	borrowed	he was _____
to follow	_____	she _____ following
to stroll	_____	I was _____
_____	smiled	you were _____

B Complete these sentences by adding **past tense verbs**.

1 I _____ _____ when it began to snow.

2 We _____ _____ when we saw the accident.

3 She _____ _____ all day.

4 He _____ _____ breakfast when the post came.

27

Nouns

Possessive nouns tell you who owns something. They have an apostrophe **'** and an **s** at the end.

Ruth's bicycle
Ruth is the owner.
'Ruth's bicycle' means the same as 'the bicycle belonging to Ruth'.
Ruth's is the **possessive noun**.

Roger's book
Roger is the owner.
'Roger's book' means the same as 'the book belonging to Roger'.
Roger's is the **possessive noun**.

The **'s** tells you who or what is the owner.

GRAMMAR *Focus*

Copy the following into your book.
Underline the name of the **owner** in each one.

1 Deepak's football
2 the girl's laugh
3 the flower's stem
4 the doctor's coat
5 the dog's lead
6 the car's engine
7 Nigel's shoe
8 the farmer's field
9 the captain's ship
10 the boy's hair

Copy the sentences below.
Add an **apostrophe** to the name of the owner in each sentence.

1 Garys homework was very hard.

2 Graham found the dogs lead in the park.

3 That mans tie has red and blue spots.

4 The cats claws were very sharp.

5 In the autumn, that trees leaves fall off.

6 The books cover was torn.

7 The reporters notebook was in her pocket.

8 Nadias wish came true.

9 Tamara didn't like Amandas coat.

10 The old mans gloves were lost.

A Write these in a shorter way, using **possessive nouns**.

1 the hand belonging to the girl

2 the dinner belonging to the boy

3 the tail belonging to the mouse

4 the song belonging to the bird

5 the wheels belonging to the tractor

B Write five sentences of your own, using a **possessive noun** in each one.

29

Sentences

A sentence has two parts.
The **subject** is the thing or person that the sentence is about.
The **predicate** is the rest of the sentence.

A sentence needs a capital letter and a full stop or a question mark.

Subject	Predicate
The eagle	is a large bird.
My bucket	has a hole in it.
Rabbits	live in burrows.
I	would like a kitten.

GRAMMAR *Focus*

A Copy the following sentences into your book.
Underline the **subject** in each sentence.

1 I have hurt my knee.

2 Sharks live in the sea.

3 The Queen lives in a palace.

4 The horses are in the stable.

B Copy the sentences below.
Underline the **predicate** in each sentence.

1 The bakery opens at nine o' clock.

2 We decided to go to the park.

3 The river burst its banks.

4 Our garage is big enough for two cars.

Join each **subject** with the right **predicate** to make a sentence.
Write the five sentences in your book.

Subject	**Predicate**
1 The cottage	watched the match.
2 I	was very exciting.
3 The race	was near the stream.
4 A large crowd	wrote the answers carefully.
5 Sam	am paddling a canoe.

GRAMMAR *Extension*

A Write an interesting **subject** for each of these predicates.

1 _____ fell into the pond.

2 _____ were afraid of the dark.

3 _____ frightened my brother.

4 _____ left her bag on the bus.

B Write an interesting **predicate** for each of these subjects.

1 The rotting apple _____ .

2 The huge forest _____ .

3 They _____ .

4 Some birds _____ .

Verbs

Verbs tell us what action is happening.

The **tense** of a verb tells us when an action happened.

If the action is happening in the present, we use the **present tense**.

> She knits a jumper.
> or
> She is knitting a jumper.

If the action happened in the past, we use the **past tense**.

> He climbed the mountain.
> or
> He was climbing the mountain.

If we want to write about what is going to happen in the future, we use the **future tense**.

The future tense is made up of two parts:

Part 1: **shall** after **I** and **we**

       will after **you**, **he**, **she**, **it** and **they**

Part 2: the verb family name.

> I shall swim to the steps.
> She will dive into the pool.

GRAMMAR *Focus*

Copy the following sentences into your book.
Underline the **future tense verbs**.

1 I shall go at seven o'clock.

2 If it rains, we will take an umbrella.

3 He will wrap the present in a minute.

4 The children will know when to sing.

5 We shall catch the bus to town.

A Copy the sentences below.
Change the **present tense verbs** to the **future tense**.

1 Sanjay answers the question.

2 Mandy is paying for the apples.

3 We are walking to school.

B Copy the sentences below.
Change the **past tense verbs** to the **future tense**.

1 Freddy strolled along the beach.

2 The teacher was talking to the class.

3 The cars raced around the track.

GRAMMAR *Extension*

A Copy this table and fill in the missing words.

Verb family name	Present tense	Past tense	Future tense
to believe	I believe	I believed	I shall believe
to _____	they argue	they _____	they _____ _____
to work	she _____	she _____	she _____ _____
to _____	we notice	we _____	we _____ _____

If we want to make a strong statement, we put **will** after
I and **we**, and **shall** after **you, he, she, it** and **they**.

I **will** not eat that cabbage!
You **shall** eat this meal!

B Put *shall* or *will* in each gap to make these into strong
statements.

1 You _____ go to bed at nine o'clock!

2 I _____ ride my bike down the lane!

3 He _____ not go to the pictures!

Nouns and verbs

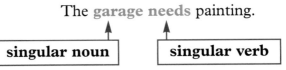

Nouns can be **singular** or **plural**.
Verbs can also be **singular** or **plural**.

When we use a singular noun, we must also use a singular verb.

The **garage needs** painting.

| singular noun | singular verb |

When we use a plural noun, we must use a plural verb.

The **garages need** painting.

| plural noun | plural verb |

English can be very strange! When we want a plural noun, we usually add **s**, **es** or **ies**. When we want a plural verb, we usually take off the **s**.

The verb families '**to be**' and '**to have**' can be tricky. Learn these:

	Present tense singular	plural	Past tense singular	plural
To be	I am you are he is she is it is	we are you are they are	I was you were he was she was it was	we were you were they were
To have	I have you have he has she has it has	we have you have they have	I had you had he had she had it had	we had you had they had

GRAMMAR *Focus*

Copy the following sentences into your book.
Choose the correct **verb** to finish each one.

1   The cottages is/are empty.

2   We is/are going to buy them.

3   I is/am going to live in one of them.

A Put each of these nouns into a sentence, followed by *have* or *has*.

1 crowd   2 children   3 team

4 girls   5 mice   6 everyone

7 oxen   8 herd   9 women

B Copy the sentences below.
Choose the correct **verb** to finish each one.

1 The cake crumble/crumbles when you cut it.

2 The icing is/are very soft.

3 I like/likes to eat this cake.

4 We buy/buys this cake every week.

GRAMMAR *Extension*

Copy this passage, correcting the mistakes.

We goes to the library on a Saturday morning. I likes to read adventure stories but my sister like books about animals. We takes three books home every week. The man in the library are very helpful. If he haven't got the book I wants, he order it for next time.

35

Singular and plural

Singular nouns are made **plural** in different ways:

	Singular	Plural
For most nouns, we add an **s**.	jacket	jacke**ts**
For nouns ending in **s**, **ch**, **sh** and **x**, we add **es**.	class	class**es**
For some nouns ending in **y**, we take off the **y** and add **ies**.	family	famil**ies**
For nouns ending in **y** with a vowel in front of the **y**, we add **s**.	trolley	trolley**s**
For nouns ending in **o**, we usually add **es**.	tomato	tomato**es**
For musical nouns ending in **o** and for nouns ending in **oo**, we just add **s**.	cello bamboo	cello**s** bamboo**s**

Some nouns do not follow any of these rules.
They have a plural that is a different word, for example:

Singular	Plural
child	children
goose	geese
person	people

GRAMMAR *Focus*

A Make these singular nouns **plural**.
Write the plurals in your book.

1 photo	2 piano	3 potato
4 hippo	5 cockatoo	6 piccolo

B Make these singular nouns **plural**.
You can use a dictionary to help you.

1 woman	2 tooth	3 ox
4 foot	5 mouse	6 postman

A Copy the sentences.
Write *is* or *are* to finish each sentence.

1 The video _____ being mended.

2 The mice _____ chewing through the rope.

3 The hippos _____ playing in the mud.

4 The oxen _____ working in the field.

B Copy the sentences.
Write *was* or *were* to finish each sentence.

1 The children _____ having tea.

2 This man _____ a farmer.

3 The cockatoos _____ colourful birds.

4 The geese _____ swimming on the pond.

GRAMMAR *Extension*

A Use a dictionary to find the **plural** of these nouns.

1 cod	2 trout	3 salmon
4 mackerel	5 sheep	6 deer

B Some words are always plural.

Write the names of the pictures in your book.

1 _____ 2 _____ 3 _____ 4 _____

Check-up 2

Singular and plural

Write the **plurals** of these nouns.

1	calf	2	life	3	loaf	4	gulf
5	dwarf	6	knife	7	thief	8	cliff
9	goose	10	piano	11	mouse	12	deer

Adjectives

A Write the **comparative** of each adjective.

1	calm	2	loud	3	bumpy	4	sleepy
5	funny	6	marvellous	7	white	8	terrifying

B Write the **superlative** of each adjective.

1	happy	2	lonely	3	hard	4	ancient
5	dirty	6	dangerous	7	muddy	8	enjoyable

Verbs

Copy the sentences.
Underline the **past tense verb** in each sentence.

1 The clown was tumbling in the ring.
2 We quickly scrambled up the hill.
3 Rita strolled to the shops.
4 The children were grumbling all the time.
5 I was working hard all day.

Nouns

A Copy the sentences.
Underline the **owner** in each sentence.

1 The dog's ball was lost in the bushes.
2 Maisie's umbrella was bright yellow.
3 The manager's car had broken down.
4 The giraffe's neck is very long.
5 The giant's feet are enormous.

B Copy these sentences.
In each sentence, add the **apostrophe** to the owner's name.

1 The ghosts scream was frightening.

2 The alligators teeth were very sharp.

3 The kittens fur is very soft.

C Write these in a shorter way, using **possessive nouns**.

1 the skirt of Tina

2 the birthday present of Bill

3 the car of Mum

4 the tail of the rat

5 the birthday of Julie

Sentences

A Copy these sentences.
Underline the **subject** in each sentence.

1 I catch a bus to school every day.

2 Swallows fly south for the winter.

3 The icy path was very dangerous.

B Finish these sentences with interesting **predicates**.

1 The old wreck _____ .

2 My younger brother _____ .

3 The grey clouds _____ .

Nouns and verbs

Correct these sentences.

1 My friend and I is going for a walk.

2 Everyone have gone out.

3 My sister were in the school choir.

4 The mice lives in the barn.

Nouns

All nouns are naming words.

There are many different types of **nouns**.

Common nouns tell us the names of ordinary things.

match   **table**   **box**

Proper nouns tell us the names of special things.

Mr Price   **India**   **Sunday**

Collective nouns tell us the names of groups of things.

a flock of sheep   **a bunch of grapes**

Compound nouns are made by joining two nouns together.

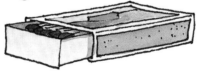 

matchbox   **tablecloth**

GRAMMAR *Focus*

In your book, write the **compound noun** for each of these pictures.

1 _____ 2 _____ 3 _____ 4 _____

Join each noun from the first box with a noun from the second box to make a **compound noun**.

space	lace
egg	ship
rain	cup
neck	coat
door	mark
book	step

GRAMMAR *Extension*

A Make a list of the **compound nouns** you can find in this passage.

It was the day of the important football match. Sally was excited because she had been chosen as the team goalkeeper. She was so excited that she had forgotten to do her homework and her schoolteacher was not pleased. At twelve o'clock the team went out. They walked along a footpath to get to the pitch. Sally put her tracksuit by the sideline and waited for the match to begin.

B Use these **compound nouns** in sentences of your own.

1 flowerbed   2 hillside   3 daylight
4 housework   5 waterfall   6 stairway

Adverbs

An **adverb** tells us more about **how, when** or **where** the action of a verb takes place.

How?	Sam clapped **loudly**.
When?	Mandy fell off her bicycle **yesterday**.
Where?	I put the flowers **outside**.

Some adverbs tell us more about other adverbs.

I walked **very quickly** to catch the bus.

It rained **quite heavily** during the night.

We can use **comparative** and **superlative** adverbs to compare actions, just as we use adjectives to compare nouns.

We add the words '**more**' and '**most**' for adverbs ending in **ly**.

Comparative adverbs compare two things. **Superlative adverbs** compare three or more things.

Adverb	Comparative	Superlative
quickly	more quickly	most quickly
clearly	more clearly	most clearly
loudly	more loudly	most loudly

We add **er** and **est** to adverbs that do not end in **ly**.

Adverb	Comparative	Superlative
hard	hard**er**	hard**est**
high	high**er**	high**est**

Some adverbs don't follow this pattern and we have to learn them.

Be careful!
A few adverbs do not follow these rules.

Adverb	Comparative	Superlative
well	better	best
badly	worse	worst

GRAMMAR *Focus*

In your book write the **comparatives** and **superlatives** of these adverbs.

| 1 easily | 2 happily | 3 patiently | 4 early |
| 5 seriously | 6 late | 7 widely | 8 badly |

A Write these sentences, changing the brown **adverbs** into **comparatives**.

1 When it snows we will be able to use the sledge often.

2 The donkeys trotted quickly when it began to rain.

3 The vegetables grew well after we watered them.

B Change the brown **adverb** into a **superlative** in each sentence.

1 Ben tried hard and won the race.

2 The last choir to perform was tuneful.

3 You have scored badly in the test.

GRAMMAR *Extension*

The second brown word in each sentence gives you a clue to the adverb you need.

A Replace each brown word with a **single adverb**.

1 The nurse dealt with the emergency with calmness.

2 Sam dribbled the ball with skill.

3 Lisa answered the question with truth.

B Use these **comparative** and **superlative** adverbs in sentences of your own.

1 worse   2 more dishonestly

3 widest   4 most clearly

5 more neatly   6 earliest

Contractions

An apostrophe '
replaces the missing
letter or letters in a
contraction.

Contractions are words that have been made smaller by missing out letters.

I am = **I'm**   you are = **you're**

We usually use contractions when we are speaking or when we are writing direct speech.

"**That's** not right," explained John. "A rectangle **doesn't** have five corners."

That's = that is   **doesn't** = does not

GRAMMAR *Focus*

A In your book, write these **contractions** in full.

1 who's	2 they'll	3 he's
4 you're	5 doesn't	6 there's
7 who'd	8 shouldn't	9 we've

B Write the **contractions** for these pairs of words.

1 would not	2 have not	3 she has
4 we are	5 we shall	6 has not
7 who would	8 will not	9 let us

Copy this conversation, changing the green words into **contractions**.

"I cannot find my book anywhere," shouted Justin. "I have seen it in my room but it is not there now."

"If you would put things away you would be able to find them," said his mother. "I shall come and help you when I have finished writing this letter."

"I shall ask Trevor," said Justin. "He will know where it is. I bet he has got it."

A Write the **contraction** from each of the sentences below.
Next to it, write the two words that it replaces.

1 "The ball's gone into the pond," shouted Philip.

2 "We'll need a long stick to get it out," said Luke.

3 "I'll go and look in the shed," said Philip.

Remember to use inverted commas for direct speech.

B Write a conversation between two or three people, using as many of the following **contractions** as you can.

can't	he'll	she's	haven't
it's	they've	won't	don't

45

UNIT 20

Nouns

If there is only one owner, the noun is singular. If there is more than one owner, the noun is plural.

A **possessive noun** tells us who owns something.

When there is only one owner, we add an **'s** to the noun.

the tiger's roar

the baby's rattle

Where there is more than one owner, we add **'** if there is already an **s** at the end, or **'s** if there is not already an **s** at the end.

the boys' sledges

the cats' tails

the children's hats

the oxen's tails

GRAMMAR *Focus*

Write the following examples in your book.
Add the **apostrophes** to show the owners.
All the owners are singular.

1 the churchs spire

2 the mans gloves

3 the birds nest

4 the clocks hands

5 Barrys shed

6 the girls idea

7 Susans face

8 the teapots spout

9 the buckets handle

10 the videos box

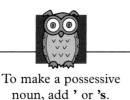

To make a possessive noun, add ' or 's.

Change the examples below by using **possessive nouns**.
All the owners are plural.
The first one has been done for you.

1 the hideout of the thieves

the thieves' hideout

2 the meeting of the parents

3 the homework of the children

4 the headlines of the newspapers

5 the race of the men

6 the mothers of the girls

7 the trunks of the trees

8 the belts of the coats

GRAMMAR *Extension*

A Copy the sentences below.
Carefully decide if the owner is singular or plural.
Add the **apostrophe** to the owner or owners.

1 The twins birthday is in January.

2 The policemans helmet fell on the ground.

3 The policemens uniforms were blue.

4 Mr Taylors house is being decorated.

5 The childrens school was broken into.

6 My three sisters bedroom is always a mess.

B Use these **plural possessive nouns** in sentences of your own.

1 ships' 2 cousins' 3 women's

4 libraries' 5 friends' 6 curtains'

7 farmers' 8 passengers' 9 teams'

Adjectives

Adjectives describe and compare nouns.

We can describe a jumper using an **adjective**.

    a **dirty** jumper

We can compare two jumpers using a **comparative adjective**.

    a dirty jumper   a **dirtier** jumper

We can compare three or more jumpers using a **superlative adjective**.

    a dirty jumper a dirtier jumper   the **dirtiest** jumper

A few adjectives change completely in their comparative and superlative forms. You need to learn them.

Adjective	Comparative	Superlative
bad	worse	worst
good	better	best
little	less	least
much	more	most
many	more	most
some	more	most

GRAMMAR *Focus*

Choose the correct **adjective** to complete each sentence. Write the sentences in your book.

1 This is the *better/best* birthday party I have ever had.

2 You can get *more/most* water in this jug than in that one.

3 Today's weather made it the *worse/worst* day of the holiday.

Copy this table and fill in the missing words.

Comparative adjectives can be made by adding **er**, **ier** or '**more**'. Superlative adjectives can be made by adding **est**, **iest** or '**most**'.

Adjective	Comparative	Superlative
silly	_____	silliest
formal	more formal	_____ _____
good	_____	_____
beautiful	_____ _____	most beautiful
_____	less	_____
_____	_____	happiest
wonderful	_____ _____	_____ _____
_____	merrier	_____
some	_____	_____
_____	_____	worst
_____	more comfortable	_____ _____
new	_____	_____
old	_____	_____
_____	_____	wisest

Write sentences using the following **adjectives**.

1 the comparative of **important**
2 the superlative of **good**
3 the superlative of **frightening**
4 the comparative of **small**
5 the comparative of **some**
6 the superlative of **bad**
7 the superlative of **sleepy**
8 the comparative of **heavy**

Sentences

Sentences have two parts.
The **subject** is the thing or person written about.
The **predicate** is the rest of the sentence.

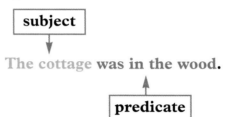

The cottage **was in the wood.**

This is a very simple sentence that does not tell us very much. It is not very interesting.
We can make the sentence more interesting by adding to the **subject**.

subject

The old, tumbledown cottage was in the wood.

We can make the sentence even more interesting by adding to the **predicate**.

The old, tumbledown cottage **was in the dark, gloomy wood.**

predicate

We have added **adjectives** to the subject and the predicate to make the sentences more interesting.

GRAMMAR *Focus*

Copy these sentences into your book.
Underline the **subject** of each sentence in blue and the **predicate** in red.

1 The pillow was on the bed.

2 I like to go to the pictures.

3 The priest wore a cloak.

4 The battery was flat.

5 Robin is cooking the dinner.

A Copy each sentence. Underline the **subject**
Write each sentence again, making the **subject** more interesting.

1 The butterfly sat on a leaf.

2 Monkeys live in the jungle.

3 A package was delivered.

B Copy each sentence. Underline the **predicate**.
Write each sentence again, making the **predicate** more interesting.

1 The flag was hoisted up the pole.

2 I went to the shop.

3 Rafique has a bicycle.

I is used as the **subject** of a sentence.

I am doing my homework.

⬆

    subject

Me is used in the **predicate** of a sentence.

Mum is taking me to the match.

⬆

    predicate

Complete these sentences by adding *I* or *me*.

1 _____ saw a ghost in the old house.

2 Will you get _____ a drink?

3 Katy and _____ are going swimming.

4 The dog frightened Becky and _____.

Sentences

Direct speech is when we write the actual words that someone has spoken.

I feel cold.

We use **inverted commas** to show the actual words spoken.

"I feel cold," said Nick.

We begin a new line when a different person speaks.

"I feel cold," said Nick.
"So do I," replied Maggie.

After the spoken words, you need some punctuation. Usually we use a comma.

"I feel cold," said Tom.

We can also use a question mark.

"Do you feel cold?" asked Mum.

We can also use an exclamation mark.

"I'm frozen!" shouted the boy.

The punctuation after the spoken words always comes **before** the inverted commas.

GRAMMAR *Focus*

Copy the following sentences into your book.
Put **inverted commas** around the spoken words.

1 The police are coming soon, said Anne.

2 What is the time? asked Richard.

3 Watch out! yelled the farmer.

4 Don't make any noise, whispered the girl.

5 I'm bored, complained Bridget.

GRAMMAR *Practice*

Copy the sentences below.
Put in any missing **punctuation**.

1 Grab this rope shouted the climber

2 May I have an apple asked Tara

3 That building over there is the museum said the guide

4 I have lost my purse sobbed Kathy

5 Have you got your ticket asked the bus driver

GRAMMAR *Extension*

Sometimes the words that tell us who is speaking come before the spoken words.

    Dad said, "You can watch a video tonight."

We always divide the spoken words from the words telling us who is speaking with a comma.

    The boy mumbled, "I don't know the answer."
    The teacher said, "Please learn it for tomorrow."

Put in the missing punctuation –
inverted commas, full stops, commas, question marks and exclamation marks.

Copy the sentences below.
Put in the missing **punctuation**.

1 Where is the treasure hidden asked the pirate

2 Billy said I have got the map

3 Let me see it demanded the pirate

4 Billy asked What will you give me in return

5 With a cruel laugh, the pirate replied Nothing

6 That's not fair gasped Billy

53

Verbs

Verbs tell us what is happening.

The **tense** of a verb tells us when something happens – in the **past**, in the **present** or in the **future**.

We usually make the **past tense** by adding **d** or **ed** to the verb family name.

   Hannah talk**ed** to her friend.

Some verbs have **irregular** past tenses.

   Hannah **told** him about her holiday.

We can also make the **past tense** by using the verb '**to be**' and an **ing** word.

   She **was talking** to her friend.

We make the **present tense** by using the **verb family name** or the verb '**to be**' and an **ing** word.

   I **walk** to school.
or I **am walking** to school.

We make the **future tense** by using the verb '**to be**' and the **verb family name**.

   I **will go** at ten o'clock.

> Remember, if we are using he, she or it in the present tense, we add 's' to the verb family name.

GRAMMAR *Focus*

Copy this table into your book.
Fill in the missing **verb tenses**.

Family name	Past tense	Present tense	Future tense
to walk	I walked I was walking	I walk I am walking	I shall walk
to grow	he _____ he _____ _____	he _____ he _____ _____	he _____ _____
to bring	you _____ you _____ _____	you _____ you _____ _____	you _____ _____
to see	we _____ we _____ _____	we _____ we _____ _____	we _____ _____

GRAMMAR *Practice*

Copy the sentences below.
After each sentence write whether it is **past tense**, **present tense** or **future tense**.

1 I am sewing seven buttons on to my jacket.
2 The army wore bright red uniforms.
3 Your helmet will protect you.
4 She was making a cake when the doorbell rang.
5 I believe everything you say.

GRAMMAR *Extension*

A Write these sentences in the **past tense**.

1 My neighbour is working in the garden.
2 This is a valuable vase.
3 The giant is frightening the villagers.
4 The dog steals the sausages.
5 I go to the shops every morning.

B Write these sentences in the **future tense**.

1 The siren sounded at midnight.
2 It happens every day at four o'clock.
3 I ate my tea very quickly.
4 The dog washes her new puppies.
5 The match was cancelled because of the bad weather.

Sentences

Contractions which end in **n't** and the words **no**, **not**, **nothing**, **never** and **nowhere** are **negative** words.

By using these words, we can change the meaning of a sentence.

He has an ice cream.   He **does not** have an ice cream.
Positive   **Negative**

When two negative words are used in the same sentence, it is called a **double negative**.

If there are two negative words in one sentence, they cancel each other out and the meaning becomes positive.

I do **not** have **no** money.   Two negatives = positive

The two negative words make the sentence mean 'I do have some money.'
The correct sentence would be:

I do **not** have any money.

GRAMMAR *Focus*

Add a **negative word** to each sentence to make it mean the opposite.
Write the sentences in your book.

1 I _____ have an apple for lunch.

2 She has _____ time to tidy her room.

3 The children do _____ want to go to the park.

4 There is _____ space in the cupboard.

5 I _____ lift this heavy box.

6 Greg _____ goes to the library on Saturday.

Copy the sentences below.
Underline the **negative** words.
Write the sentences again, so that they have the opposite meaning.

1 The thief said he knew nothing about the burglary.

2 He did not have a ticket to get in.

3 The boys had nowhere to go.

4 "I mustn't feed the cat," said Dad.

GRAMMAR *Extension*

A Write the **contractions** of these **negative words**.

1 cannot	2 will not	3 shall not
4 must not	5 have not	6 should not
7 would not	8 does not	9 do not
10 is not	11 could not	12 has not

B All these sentences have **two negative words**, so they do not mean what the writer intended.
Write each sentence again so that it means what the writer wanted.
The first one has been done for you.

1 I wanted to win the race but I didn't have no luck.

I wanted to win the race but I didn't have any luck.

2 Pam didn't want to go nowhere.

3 I mustn't throw nothing away.

4 Mum will not get no bus today.

Nouns

Nouns are naming words.

There are several types of **nouns**.
Most nouns are names of things you can see and touch.

There are **common nouns**.

a **camera**

There are **proper nouns**.

Mr Philips

There are **collective nouns**.

a **shoal** of fish

There are **compound nouns**.

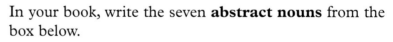

a **notebook**

Abstract nouns are the names of things you cannot touch, taste, smell or hear.
They are the names of:

Qualities	bravery	heroism	stupidity
Feelings	fear	happiness	anger
Times	evening	Wednesday	holiday

GRAMMAR *Focus*

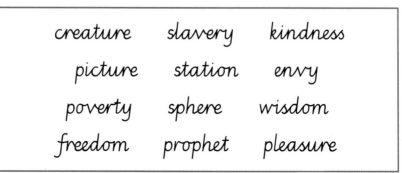

In your book, write the seven **abstract nouns** from the box below.

creature	slavery	kindness
picture	station	envy
poverty	sphere	wisdom
freedom	prophet	pleasure

Copy the sentences below.
Underline the **common noun** and the **abstract noun** in each sentence.

1 Fear made the boy cry.

2 Everyone admired his talent.

3 That concert gave me great pleasure.

4 The old woman lived in poverty.

GRAMMAR *Extension*

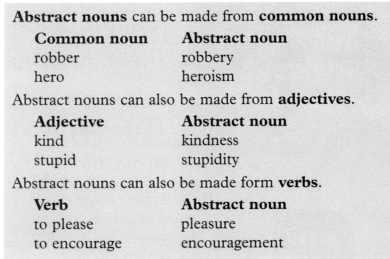

Abstract nouns can be made from **common nouns**.

Common noun	Abstract noun
robber	robbery
hero	heroism

Abstract nouns can also be made from **adjectives**.

Adjective	Abstract noun
kind	kindness
stupid	stupidity

Abstract nouns can also be made form **verbs**.

Verb	Abstract noun
to please	pleasure
to encourage	encouragement

A Copy the **common nouns** below.
Write the **abstract nouns** that can be made from them.

1 *infant* 2 *friend* 3 *thief*

B Copy the **adjectives** below.
Write the **abstract nouns** that can be made from them.

1 *skilful* 2 *famous* 3 *active*

C Copy the **verbs** below.
Write the **abstract nouns** that can be made from them.

1 *to deceive* 2 *to free* 3 *to flatter*

Check-up 3

Proper nouns

Write these film titles correctly.

1 *gone with the wind*

2 *mary poppins*

3 *the hunchback of notre dame*

Adjectives

A Copy the sentences below.
Underline the **number order adjectives**.

1 *Astronauts landed on the Moon in the twentieth century.*

2 *That is the second time I have warned you.*

3 *The family gave Dad a surprise party on his thirty-fifth birthday.*

B Write the **comparative** and the **superlative** of each of these adjectives.

1 loud	2 immense	3 bad
4 shabby	5 good	6 tidy
7 little	8 terrifying	9 important
10 honest	11 much	12 kind
13 many	14 grumpy	15 some

Singular and plural

Write the **plurals** of these nouns.

1 pony	2 foot	3 loaf
4 piano	5 donkey	6 baby
7 banjo	8 half	9 wharf
10 scarf	11 berry	12 tooth

Prepositions

Copy the sentences below.
Underline the **preposition** in each sentence.

1 The rat hid behind the shed.

2 The ball was thrown over the fence.

3 I went into the shop to buy some bread.

4 The tree was growing near the water.

Sentences

A Copy the sentences below.
Underline the **subject** in each sentence.

1 This door needs painting.

2 I have hurt my leg.

3 The noisy children were chasing
each other.

4 The violent storm frightened the animals.

B Copy the sentences below.
Underline the **object** in each sentence.

1 I would like a banana.

2 The torn umbrella did not keep off
the rain.

3 All the books have colourful covers.

4 We need to mend the gate.

C Add interesting **predicates** to complete these sentences.

1 The lonely man _____.

2 Every flower _____.

3 The two goats _____.

4 These shabby curtains _____.

D Copy the sentences below and add the missing **punctuation**.

1 I will carry that for you offered Jake

2 Will you come for tea asked Danny

3 Mark said I can't find my jumper

4 Elizabeth shouted Look out

Pronouns

Use these **pronouns** in sentences of your own.

1 myself 2 yourself 3 ourselves

4 itself 5 himself 6 herself

7 yourselves 8 themselves

Collective nouns

A Write a **collective noun** for each of these.

1 soldiers 2 flowers 3 books

4 geese 5 lions 6 birds

7 musicians 8 sheep 9 cows

B Join each noun from the first box with a noun from the second box to make a **compound noun**.

rain	shade
fire	light
sun	man
sea	drop
day	shore

C Copy these sentences.
Add the **apostrophe** to the owner or owners.

1 The giraffes neck is long and thin.

2 Where is this childs coat?

3 Birds feathers help them to fly.

D Copy the sentences below.
Underline the **abstract nouns**.

1 The pain in my arm made me cry.

2 The escape was planned for midnight.

3 "My memory is not what it used to be," said Mum.

4 It's a mystery where that book has gone.

E Use these **abstract nouns** in sentences of your own.

1 generosity 2 joy   3 pain

4 misery   5 knowledge 6 wisdom

Verbs

A Copy the sentences below.
Use the **past tense** – the verb '**to be**' and **ing** – instead of the verb family name.

1 I to talk to my friend when the telephone rang.

2 She to run for the bus when she tripped.

3 Sam to post a letter when it began to rain.

4 I did my homework while my brother to read his book.

B Write these sentences as though they will happen in the **future**.

1 The candle burned all night.

2 The bells jingled in the wind.

3 I listen to the radio on Saturday morning.

4 The cabbage is rotting in the vegetable basket.

5 The palace was built of stone.

C Copy and correct these sentences.

1 The children goes to the park to play.
2 Ben find his ball in the long grass.
3 I wants my tea now.
4 Cats likes milk to drink.
5 The foal gallop around the field.

Contractions

Copy the sentences below.
Add the **apostrophes** to the **contractions**.

1 "I cant go out this evening," said Debbie.
2 "We wont get there in time if we dont hurry," said Mum.
3 "Sharon mustnt leave her book at home again," said the teacher.
4 "Why shouldnt you cross the road here?" asked the policewoman.
5 "I couldnt do the long jump and I wouldnt do the high jump," said Megan.

Double negatives

Write these sentences again so they say what the writer wanted.

1 Hamish did not get no lunch today.
2 I never go nowhere on a Sunday.
3 The boys couldn't find nowhere to play.
4 The cat didn't climb no trees in the park.
5 Can't I not go out today?